So,

You Want A Job?

Hah!

Don't Make Me Laugh!

Mamie Butler Gadson

MAMIE BUTLER GADSON

Dedication

This book is dedicated to every job seeker who

Wants a job offer,

Wants to be prepared,

Eagerly aspires to succeed.

So, You Want A Job? Hah! Don't Make Me Laugh!

Contents

DEDICATION

ACKNOWLEDGMENT

A WORD FROM THE AUTHOR

MS. WILLIAMS   1

MOM AND THE VETERINARIAN   11

CRUSHED ICE AND A PAPER CUP   17

MONEY AND MORE MONEY!   23

BASHER AND HER SUPERVISOR   30

CONCLUSION   35

ABOUT THE AUTHOR   40

ACKNOWLEDGMENTS

I give much affection to my husband for his unwavering belief in me, and whose inspiration has been steadfast. I would like to acknowledge my family, whom I love unconditionally, as well as friends and colleagues who relentlessly and enduringly were my sounding boards. Special thank you to Brandy Gardner, who helped this endeavor to launch. Thanks to all for your encouragement and support.

A Time for Everything

"There is a time for everything
and a season for every activity under the heavens:
a time to be born and a time to die,
a time to plant and a time to uproot,
a time to kill and a time to heal,
a time to tear down and a time to build,
a time to weep and a time to laugh,
a time to mourn and a time to dance,
a time to scatter stones and a time to gather them,
a time to embrace and a time to refrain from embracing,
a time to search and a time to give up,
a time to keep and a time to throw away,
a time to tear and a time to mend,
a time to be silent and a time to speak,
a time to love and a time to hate,
a time for war and a time for peace."

Ecclesiastes 3:1-8 (NIV)

A Word From the Author

Job seekers come in many varieties. They are, to coin a phrase, *like a box of chocolates*. In certain measure, each is intrinsically different and presents unique challenges in interviewing. And, as a former hiring manager, that's the rub that made my job so enjoyable.

Preparing for interviewing requires time and efficient planning. Regrettably, job seekers make the mistake of relying on textbook-readied answers. Then they enter an interview inadequately prepared and poorly rehearsed; which actually could work, if, they were dealing with an inexperienced hiring manager! In reality, candidates flounder headlong into an interview only to fail because they are so ill-prepared. Hiring managers skillfully craft thought-out interview questions for the sole intent of flushing out a candidate's capabilities. These questions are designed to specifically determine how proficiently candidates think or how they would handle specific behavioral situations. So without adequate preparation, a successful outcome is unlikely.

Through the lens of some hiring managers, at times, it's just plain entertaining to watch a candidate's body language as she or he succumbs to their own inadequacies. For example, when candidates cannot respond to the tough questions, simply because they did not properly prepare, they're thinking "Wow, where did that come from?!!" Next, in desperation, they search for a plausible, or, at the very least, sensible response that would not blow the interview. So how a candidate reacts to tough questions can lead to success, or it can be a deal breaker. In contrast, there are some candidates who indeed prepare very smartly, methodically, and do the research. Preparation equips them to formulate questions for use in the interview, which can only lead to a better understanding of the position for which they are applying. Naturally, this definitely results in a more productive interview.

Now, there's another type candidate! And preparation or not, it makes no difference. This candidate is considered a "hijacker". Hijackers merely show up to the interview and attempt to take charge. Research and preparation are not in their *repertoire*. They dive right in and try to navigate the interview instead of waiting for their appointed opportunity given to them by the interviewer. This candidate is wholly undisciplined. But not on my watch! A candidate cannot step into the arena, take charge of the interview, and expect a job offer. To be clear, one must understand the difference between the hiring manager and the job seeker!

Often candidates simply don't understand the protocol of job interviewing. During an interview, candidates should first posture themselves to just merely listen and pay close attention. In turn, they can actually learn information they may not have already known. For example, a candidate could learn about the employer's business successes, its culture, and above all, pertinent specifics about the job position. Now why would anyone want to miss this?!! What you don't know CAN hurt you!

The business of interviewing can wander down the path of being vastly "strange" as well as entertaining. Some interviews are truly painful, while others are just plain hilarious. "So, You Want A Job? Hah! Don't Make Me Laugh!" reveals how wrong interviews can turn based on certain behaviors and characteristics. These are basic behaviors that should have been honed before the interview and "avoided." With subtle enhancements, these are some of my stories with unprepared candidates whom I've interviewed. Although the names were changed to protect identity, these were real interviews. The job seekers actually applied for these jobs and seriously asserted they were interested in being hired. I emphatically will not say who was, or was not, hired. I'll let you be the judge! Journey with me now through these storied interviews so memorable to me. Then, determine for yourself whether the candidates would have been a good or bad hire. Having said all this, at times, I was truly forced to say, "Hah! Don't make me laugh!"

Mamie Butler Gadson

Ms. Williams

THE SEARCH WAS FOR Legal Administrative Assistant, a real self-starter, who possessed eight plus years of recent and related experience. Legal Administrative Assistants have diverse patchworks of experience often derived from various areas of legal practices. For instance, some areas of law can include corporate, litigation, finance restructuring, products liability, mass torts, intellectual property, just to name a few. With experience, assistants have the ability to support multiple attorneys. In the case of this job opening, I was seeking someone experienced in working for commercial litigation lawyers. This involved contractual disputes and money damages, class actions, business torts, civil RICO claims and a host of other legal defense practices. The expectation was that assistants possessed an understanding of procedural law for filings cases within the legal courts. The attorneys primarily focus on the side of substantive law. Attorneys are more specifically involved with legal statutes and citations in case law--mounds of legal research, client liaison, preparation of legal documents for filing with the court and personally attending court appearances--the actual practice of law! While this is not the whole ball of wax in lawyering it covers the basics. So my candidate not only needed to be highly skilled, but tough-skinned, and able to demonstrate how their experience matched the job requirements. Pretty simple, right?

On this particular day, Ms. Williams was scheduled to interview with me. There's a little story about her last name and why she's continually referred to as "Ms. Williams." The employment agency stated that she resembled Vanessa Williams, the former and first black "Miss America." I didn't care! Physical attraction wasn't a criterion or part of my interviewing ethics. All that Ms. Williams needed to possess was enough tenacity to work with three entertaining, temperamental, yet highly intelligent lawyers. Landing the job required being flexible to work long hours that sometimes extended through lunch, and on into the evening. For me to learn that the staffing agency was sending "Miss America," with perhaps a few skills thrown in the mix, seriously clouded my enthusiasm to meet the candidate. I placed myself into a state of mind prepping and purged all preconceived notions or unfair biases.

Ms. Williams arrived timely. I greeted her in the reception area and everything was off to a level playing field. Oddly, she failed in any resemblance of the star Williams. I was relieved. It saved me of having to filter through the halo effect, because of the distraction of her appearance. In addition, I applied the "thin slicing" technique, which quickly helps to assess an individual in a short period of time. On the walk to the conference room, I noted a few things about Ms. Williams. First, there was an annoying flopping noise in her steps. Ms. Williams had difficulty walking quietly because she was wearing strapless heels--of aqua blue. She had selected to wear a deep rich-looking navy suit complimented by a multicolored scarf with different hues of blue to pick up the color of her shoes. The suit was very nice. The overall combination however would not be advice found in a "What to Wear for an Interview" guide. It was her choice nonetheless. The second glaring observation was that she carried a black satchel as large as a weekender tote. Perhaps she packed many, many copies of resumes and references. Although noted, I still didn't care. I needed to hire a talented assistant and was eager to get into the interview and learn if she could do the job!

Now seated at the conference table, I thanked Ms. Williams for coming to interview for the position. I shared firm history, reflected upon the fact that diversity was the genesis of what had become a robust and prominent law firm. To this point, I had really done all the talking. It was a way of easing into the discussion and then finally bringing the candidate into the conversation. "Ms. Williams, before moving forward, I just want to mention that at some point our managing partner may stop in to meet you as well. So don't be alarmed." Demurely, Ms. William replied "Ok." It was the second time I'd heard her voice since our greeting. "Very soft," I thought. I needed a person of supreme confidence—firmness. "Great, then let's get started. Why don't you begin by telling me about yourself?" These series of questions make up the classic opener. It helps the candidate to open up and begin talking. Ms. Williams took me on a journey— softly. We went from her birthplace, to her placing among siblings, all the way to high school graduation, and how she was attending night college classes. Not entirely what I was expecting to hear, but my thought was that all gleaned from a candidate was information to better understand the individual. I learned she was outgoing and participatory in school activities. Notably she was in dance and the choir. I would say she was on the artsy side—very quietly! There wasn't much else there to go on.

There was a quick knock, and then the conference room door swung open widely. A tall, broad figure marched forward, with hand extended, prepared to greet both me and Ms. Williams. It was A. J. Browning, managing partner. Truthfully, A. J. wasn't just stopping to meet Ms. Williams, but merely to "check her out"! After all, she could very possibly have been hired into the section of litigation that he managed. Somehow, he'd heard about the Miss America, Vanessa Williams story. "Perhaps my assistance spoke to his assistant? Hum, I never really got clarity on that."

I stood from my chair and shook A. J.'s hand. Not so much to honor him, but out of respect for who he was and his standing in the firm. "Mr. Browning, thank you for stopping in. Please allow me to introduce Denise Williams." Ah! Yes, you're right. Her name was completely different! Not Vanessa but Denise. I explained to A. J. that Ms. Williams was interviewing for the administrative assistant position in litigation. As I gestured toward Ms. Williams and gazed upon her, shock and dismay rushed over me. Ms. William just sat there with her elbows perched on the table and hands tucked under her chin. She didn't attempt to shake A.J.'s hand or at least show interest in acknowledging his visit. In this moment, I felt she could be demonstrating she really was a "princess!" Still seated she finally offered a limp extension of her arm and shook his hand. "It's good meeting you, Ms. Williams. And good luck to you. They're a great bunch of folks in litigation. Wish you luck!" Ms. Williams uttered-softly "thank you." A. J. winced awkwardly, shot me a quick smile and said he would speak with me later, and he left. I turned to Ms. Williams in hopes she had noted her listless error and had stood! But no, the princess remained seated. Didn't she realize who had even bothered to meet her?! Hadn't I stated the managing partner may come in to meet her? He was someone who managed the firm, approved bonuses, contributed to hiring approvals, promotions, compensation, and could make working at the firm desirable, or not so desirable. He was a mover and shaker, who had graced his presence just to meet her--the king for goodness sake!

There was a lot of ground to cover with Ms. Williams. And luckily for her, I felt her resume was fairly decent enough to even bother to continue. So far she'd failed, from the reception, into the conference room, and throughout the first 10 minutes of the interview. And also to this point, she had only provided very lame background about herself, said "hello," "ok" and "thank you." Let's see if there's anything else there!

"Ms. Williams, why do you want to work for 'Delaney, Wells & Browning?'" "Well, I know the firm has a great reputation, and I want to work in a large firm environment. I also believe I could be an asset," she said. I knew she indeed had large-firm experience, but what was she looking for specifically? So I asked, "If you could create your own dream job, what would that look like?" Ms. Williams paused and asked "Truthfully?" "No," I thought, "lie so I can discredit you and quickly escort you to the elevator." I always disliked hearing an explanation beginning with "truthfully." To me, it's a given the truth will be told. However, with courtesy and professionalism, and a smile, I replied "Yes, truthfully, please." Ms. Williams let it rip! "Because I'm a single parent, I'm seeking 9 to 5 hours and working overtime wouldn't be an option for me. I also couldn't work weekends. I need to be with my kids. On the job, I sincerely want to work with team players. For example, I want to work with attorneys who will slow down, and thoroughly communicate assignments with me." And after hearing those stunning expectations, I surmised that

Ms. Williams wanted "busy," "highly-paid lawyers," to "s-l-o-w down," and "be patient," while they all came together for moments of kumbaya and explain everything! Hah, Hah! Don't Make Me Laugh!

Clearly, her concern to put her children first was very valid. Yet, I knew I had a problem. And, I didn't want to hear about her marital status, or about her children, or religion, or any Title VII information! Even more troubling was hearing Ms. Williams say she didn't want to work overtime. This was a specific requirement of the position for which she was applying. Working overtime is *de rigueur* to the success of attorneys' law practice and to appropriately represent clients. Hearing an experienced senior, legal administrative assistant was not willing to work overtime was nonsensical. "Ms. Williams, one of the requirements of doing the job as an administrative assistant at Delaney, Wells & Browning is being flexible to work overtime as needed." In one fell swoop, she responded "Well, I simply can't. I believe with what I have to offer as well as an efficient working style that overtime wouldn't be necessary." That was it—game over! Ms. Williams wasn't hearing me. No further time needed to be taken with Ms. Williams. She had simply shot herself in the foot. Unfortunately, we never reached a discussion about her capabilities, ethics, or what she could bring to the table.

"Ms. Williams", I said, "with all due respect, not being available or unwilling to meet the basic requirement of working overtime, I believe there is no reason to go forward." Ms. Williams became flustered. "But you haven't asked about my experience. I would like to share my experience and see if my skills match what you're seeking in a candidate. I have over eight years legal experience and can do the job. I just need a chance." I sensed that desperation was setting in. But I wasn't accustomed to wasting my time or the candidate's time. It was critical that Ms. Williams felt respected and not summarily dismissed. "Ms. Williams, having critiqued your resume, I agree that you have great potential. You are going to find a job that will fit your needs and what you are seeking. As I indicated, we need someone who will have the availability and willingness to work overtime, which is a core requirement for all our administrative assistants. Based on what you have shared it is my understanding that you are either unwilling or unable to do so. Is that accurate?" That's right I'm not willing to work a lot of overtime," she said. "Well at that, Ms. Williams, I want to thank you again for spending the time to meet with me. I will walk you to the lobby." I stood from my chair and smiled. Again I said "Ms. Williams, thank you. If you will come with me, I'll walk with you to the lobby." For several seconds too long she remained seated. I wondered if she needed assistance. Finally Ms. Williams displayed she could stand. I walked to the door and continued walking. When I reached the reception area, I knew she was following by the flopping sound of her heels. Ms. Williams did not attempt to thank me or say good bye. She pivoted to the elevator, pressed "down" for the elevator and stared at the doors. Frankly, she relieved me of trying to provide additional pleasantries for which I was grateful. I returned to my office and remained optimistic the next interview would blow me away!

Mom And The Veterinarian

WHENEVER I GO TO A DOCTOR'S OFFICE or somewhere similar there are usually reminders about turning off one's cell phone. A sign reads "Clients, beyond this point, please silence and discontinue use of cell phones. Your cooperation is appreciated. Thank You." Actually this is not unreasonable. Yet while waiting, it's nice to peek at email messages or catchup on news. And I believe most people do exactly that. Once the knock at the door is heard, indicating the doctor is entering, we shut it down. So yes, no cell phone signs are practically everywhere these days. The point is there's a time and place for everything, thus Ecclesiastics 3:1-8. In so reading, it reflects how God allows everything to flow as He so purposes.

In an interview, one is expected to really make a good impression and give his or her undivided attention. Right? Yes, of course I'm right! So my candidate on this particular day is Tonya Mitchell. Tonya's resume and initial screening passed muster. I was impressed with her experience, previous work tenure, and that she was very skilled. The position for an administrative assistant required typing accuracy and the need for speed. In those days, typing test results over 100 words per minute was acceptable. Anything less, an administrative assistant probably wouldn't be able to keep pace with the demands of the job or the lawyers. The legal documents are lengthy and contain legal citations that are tedious and complicated to type. So possessing good typing skills with accuracy was the *crème de la crème* to landing a job offer. Today's legal environment doesn't have this expectation. Assistants are used differently and one's typing skill isn't a focus. Because business has gone global, assistants are tasked with duties that require them to be excellent organizers of foreign travel. Nonetheless, Tonya had great skills and had further honed her success through various administrative assistant associations. In these associations, she served in various capacities that developed her leadership and organizational abilities. To me, this displayed she possessed a strong desire to new learning experiences. She was a very promising candidate.

Tonya was punctual as this was her first test to pass. I was so excited to meet Tonya that I met her personally in the reception area. I escorted a perky individual who appeared no taller than five feet. Her slate grey suit looked impeccably smart-looking and her spectator shoes blended nicely as well. The only astonishing feature I noticed was her sense of hairstyle. A huge mass of frizzy, deeply layered waves overwhelmed her tiny frame. And the huge eyeglasses! I didn't care though. I was giddy excited to interview Tonya and ready to be impressed by all that she could bring to the table. We exchanged pleasant conversation about how terribly hot and humid Houston weather was and how the temperature had risen to 101°. Tonya apparently arrived well in advance to cool off as there were no signs of perspiration.

"Tonya, it's great to finally meet you. We've talked several times on the phone and communicated through email. It is really great that you're here and we are able to finally meet. Before we start, I would like to share some history and successes about Delany, Wills & Browning." This would give my candidate an opportunity to relax and begin to focus. I braggartly talked about the founding lawyers, the attorney and office acquisitions, domestically and internationally, and the firm's awards and rankings. I could sense my candidate wanted to be hired immediately after hearing about such an illustrious law firm.

Then something terribly amiss was happening. It was the sound of music. Any minute I expected to see Mary Poppins ascending through the air. It was music pumping ever so softly. The sound grew louder and louder. I glanced to my side and then the other side trying to discern from where this sound could possibly be coming. Ah! Yes, it was Tonya's cell phone! Her purse was next to her feet under the conference table. The timing was terrible because it was now her entrance time. She was "on," and it was her time to share her work experience and impress! This reminded me of those movie hangers when you think you're about to find out the fate of the situation only to be left to guess. Child-like, Tonya faintly smiled as if she had been discovered and was about to be assessed a penalty. She raised her index finger and whispered "one moment, excuse me just a minute, please." Internally I bristled and thought, "Really, we're doing this?" This was a serious no-no of interviewing protocol. Tonya clasped the cell phone to her ear and leaned forward as though this would better help to hear the person on the phone. "Hi Mom." There was hesitation and Tonya listened more. Then she said, "I took Tripp out this morning, Mom." Ah, don't make me laugh! Why didn't she just tell "Mom" she was in the middle of a job interview? I was anxious to hear how she would respond to my 12 very patently crafted interview questions! I asked every candidate the same questions for the same position. For instance, "How do you manage your time to ensure your work is accomplished? How do you handle stressful interactions with those whom you work? Tell me about a time when you believe you went above and beyond on the job? There were other questions to explore and my time was limited. On top of it all, other interviews were scheduled immediately after Tonya's. "No, Mom, I take Tripp to the vet on Thursday. This is Tuesday. Don't worry, Mom, I've got it under control." I couldn't believe there was a discussion going on about her dog "Tripp's" veterinarian appointment. Unbelievable! My composure switched. Both my elbows were now perched on the table, hands tucked under my chin, and I'm a little irritated. Ms. Mitchell was wasting my time. "Okay, Mom, okay. I got it. Just so you know, I'm sitting in a job interview." Ah! Finally! But her Mom didn't get it. She continued talking and Tonya kept listening. She obviously could not hang up on Mom. "I'll tell her Mom." Silence again. Then Tonya placed her hand over the mouth piece of the phone and said to me, "This is my Mom, sorry. She said to tell you hello." I suppose it was expected I would reciprocate and say hello back. I didn't and just stared at Tonya.

The remainder of time spent with Tonya was clouded. I couldn't move beyond that she wasn't strong enough to handle an interruption at such a critical time. If she could not handle a call from her mother, it was difficult to imagine how she would deal with demanding lawyers!

I sometimes wondered how different it would have been had Tonya just turned off her phone. Even had her cell phone rang, she could have quickly excused herself, reached down and shut it down. The brevity of that short intrusion may have, and that's a big maybe, been overlooked. It begs the question of how do you evaluate a person in comparison to others in this type faux pas. Nonetheless, this was exactly the result of her interview.

It's a fact that extreme optimism clearly is not always the road to success. I share this case in point, because despite optimism, it's often necessary to say "Don't call me, I'll call you." At the end of the day, I met with a candidate whose cell was turned off.

CRUSHED ICE AND A PAPER CUP

WHEN I WAS GROWING UP MY PARENTS taught me the importance of common sense. They would tell me that I could get all the education I wanted but nothing could replace common sense. It's like when a weather meteorologist says there's a ninety percent chance of precipitation, and you live in the southern coastal region of Texas, on this day, you probably need an umbrella. Now that's common sense! In employment, it's more closely referred to one having "good judgment." In the workforce, good judgment is invaluable. It's an attribute necessary in practically every capacity of work; chefs, sales persons, accountants, cashiers, teachers, police persons, nurses, assistants, mechanics, lawyers—well, I think you get the point. In this interview, we are going to see if "good judgment" or "common sense" shows-up.

17

The job opening was for a mail services clerk. The requirements were a high school diploma, six months to a year minimum experience, able to read and write and fluent in English. They needed experience receiving, sorting, filing, and delivering mail, applying postal rates, weighing and wrapping packages and various other related duties as necessary. From what I gleaned, my candidate's resume had all the requirements. It was always a sheer joy to meet a candidate whose resume reflected all the required qualifications and experience. It built anticipation and the hope of hiring the candidate. I would only have to check references and receive feedback from their previous employers. If all checked out, I had a potential new employee. Simple! Only IF she or he passed the background check.

On this day, William, my assistant, greeted the candidate for me. William was an excellent assistant. A take charge and affable type of guy. If I didn't enjoy my job as much as I did, I could have assigned any task to him and he could have handled it. I could read him well and we worked great together. William knocked on my door and his shoulder appeared to pop in first and then his head. The other part of his body remained outside the door. Oddly, he looked underwhelmed. I couldn't get a clear read. William cleared his throat and in a kooky tone said to me that Brandon Lyons was ready to meet with me in Conference Room C. All the conference rooms were named A through G. If you knew your alphabet, you knew where to be. "Thanks William," I said. "Anything I need to be aware of?" I sometimes asked William to meet the candidate just to get a sense of what he could grasp in the short time he was with them. Before I could get that out, William had returned to his workstation. If he responded, I didn't hear him. Walking out of my office I asked "William, you okay?" "Yeah, fine," he said. "Better take your drink with you." Now, William knew I never transported food or beverages into a meeting and certainly not to an interview. Hum. "Come on, William, what are you trying to tell me?" "You'll see." "Enough," I thought. I had to get to the interview to meet Brandon Lyons.

I walked to Conference Room C and entered. The scene was holy unorthodox! And for me, that's putting it lightly. I momentarily couldn't speak. Apparently Mr. Lyons had fried chicken for lunch. It was now 2:00 pm and it was still with him. Even the restaurant wrappings were there. "Hello, Brandon, I'm Mia Henderson, the hiring manager. Thank you for coming." His friendly nature was quite welcoming though. "Oh, no problem ma'am. Thank you for letting me interview." The very next thing my eyes saw was my candidate raising a paper cup to his mouth. When the cup came down, his jaws were full of ice. He continued chomping the ice until it was manageable enough to open his mouth to speak. Then I heard crackling. "Goodness gracious," I thought to myself. "And you want a job?" Hah! Don't make me laugh!

I kept my head down as though comparing his application to his resume. I thought this would give him sufficient time to finish. He twirled the cup, then picked it up, and then dropped it, and then twirled it some more all while looking at me for the next move. A stream of conscience rushed over me, and I felt the need to do an impromptu presentation on professional interviewing. But I refrained.

"Brandon, since you've had a chance to view the job description and know the expectations, why don't you tell me about your experience with your previous jobs." "Ah, sure. Ah, do you mind if I fill my cup with water first?" Seriously?!! For me this was a "first" and I thought the only right thing to do was show him to the water! "Tell you what; let me have someone bring you a glass of water. Would that be ok?" "Actually, this already has some ice in it. I asked for a lotta ice with my order. Usually people don't want a lotta ice. They want more drink. I just need to add more water." Okay, I needed to chill and just make sure he got water. After a trek up and down the hall with the water filled paper cup in hand, we returned to the conference room.

"Okay, let's get started. As I was saying, I'd like to hear about your prior employment. Let's start with your most recent job." Brandon took another sip of the water with some ice and crunched on it a little. What was his obsession with the ice! Seriously! He sat the 18 ouncer down in front of him and proceeded to respond. In the next 15 minutes we were finished. Brandon also had drunk his water and crunched on the last of the ice. He felt comfortable now to turn the cup up and pat the bottom so the remaining ice dripped in his mouth. I just ignored this. I needed to end the interview. "Brandon, I have what I need. If I have any further questions, do you mind if I give you a call? I also have a few other people to talk with. As soon as we make our decision you will hear from me—either way." "Oh, okay," he said. "Thanks. I hope to hear back," said Brandon. "You're welcome. Do you think you can find your way back to Reception?" "Yep, we've been that route already!" My sentiment exactly, I thought. Brandon shook my hand and left. He also left the empty 18 ouncer on the conference room table and the bag. It still reeked of "chicken." Hah! Don't make me laugh! Who brings a cup of ice to a job interview and an empty leftover container? At least I think it was empty. Well, maybe it did have food in it. I actually never checked.

My interview evaluation on Brandon was that he exemplified behavior during the interview that lacked good judgment that might reflect how he would make decisions in a job situation.

MONEY AND MORE MONEY

THE TIME HAD TICKED TO 2:10 PM and the candidate was late. Driving connections and traffic backup in and out of downtown Houston is notorious. The 610 Loop around the city is like a circle. Routes inside the 610 Loop have few outlets, which reliably guarantee that you will get lost. I understood this. Also a hindrance was the availability of parking. There was access to our office building's garage but the parking fees were at a premium. Because of these obstacles, I explained this to every candidate so they could plan accordingly. So my candidate obviously did not take my advice! Now it would take the candidate nearly thirty minutes to fill out the application and throw off scheduling for my next interview. Perfect! I couldn't wait to hear the excuse for my candidate being late. And, believe me, I've heard many!

Thelma Daniels, a broad woman, of fairly good height and a commanding presence, entered Conference Room G. Her gait toward me was confident and stable as she shook my hand. William introduced us and we exchanged all the initial pleasantries. I smiled at William and thanked him as always. I searched his face for any positive or negative sign. His face was blank—nothing. Apparently he was leaving me to my own discretion. From here I was ready to go into action.

"Thelma, before we get seated would you like a glass of water?" I asked. "It's terribly hot this afternoon. I can only imagine what you endured trying to get here." I was expecting this would open the conversation for her to say why she was late. If I heard what deemed a valid excuse, I was willing to give her a pass. Thelma declined the offer and said she was okay and thanked me. She gave no excuse for her late arrival. "Okay, please, have a seat." Thelma flopped down in the chair, and dropped her black and white patent leather purse on the conference table. I noted that she did have perspiration glistening across her nose and forehead. I felt she definitely needed to cool down. "Are you certain I can't get you something cool to drink?" "No, thank you. I'm fine. It's just gettin' my kids to the babysitter and all, and the ordeal of my husband and him gettin' me here was a handful for me. Got three kids and it's tough, you know?" I smiled and told her that I couldn't imagine and, in light of the time, we should get right into the interview. Besides, too much Title VII information! Nothing a hiring manager should be discussing with a candidate! I was just about to ask Thelma the first question when, as boldly as she appeared, blurted out, "How much does this job pay? The last job I worked I felt the pay was low. I need to make some real money. I have a lot of bills, you know? And right now I need to pay my rent." She paused, as though suddenly remembering something she'd forgotten to say, and ceremoniously asked, "Oh, and how often are ya'll's paydays? Is it every week?" Before I could respond, Thelma's next comment was already spilling out. "I know I ask a lot of questions, but it's important to me, you know," Thelma said. I shifted in my seat trying to understand what gave her the gumption to ask these questions. I needed to gently guide her back on track—and quickly! However, I responded to Thelma that we certainly would talk about those areas but at the moment it was a bit premature. I just wanted to get the interview launched at least!

Having made these expressions I felt I could now take the plunge and ask questions. "Thelma, let's talk now about—but Thelma began with more inquiries cutting me off. It was then I realized Thelma was high-jacking the interview! Oh my goodness!! She brought her own agenda, I thought. Thelma then announced that she didn't see the reason to talk about anything else until we got the money straight. "See, I work hard. And when I work like that, I expect a good check. Like I said, I got three kids, and my husband don't work but part-time. So you git what I'm sayin'?" I let my pen drop to the table signaling my growing impatience. Thelma shut-up, sat back, and folded her arms across her broad chest as to suggest that the next move was on me. "R-e-a-l-l-y! Is this how it's going to go?" I asked myself. I pondered what to say next. Did I tell her that we needed to discuss the job and whether we felt she could do the job? Or, did I just say to her that we were done and that it was nice meeting her? Either way, I knew in my heart it would not end well. With measured control, I asked, "Thelma, are you interested in the position? And if so, we need to discuss it." Thelma adjusted herself, shifting from one hip to the other as though she was rocking. She said "When I hear the pay, I can decide." This was irritating—no crazy! My temples were pounding and my shoulders became tensed. I resolved in my mind that it really didn't matter. And, yes, it was apparent the money was important to her. I quickly empathized that having three children and a husband earning a part-time salary had to be tough. But what was important for me, was the benefit of the firm and making a good hiring decision. The whole objective of meeting to interview was not being met. I digressed, crossed my leg, sat back, and announced to Thelma that the job paid nothing more than an hourly rate of $28.50 plus overtime. I told her we paid semi-monthly and offered competitive benefits but that's all I would discuss for the moment. I further explained that our firm salaries were comparable to the Houston market and we were an excellent firm in which to work. Thelma listened intently. She unfolded her arms and came closer, placed her hands, with fingers spread wide, on the conference table. I felt my heart was about to stop as I surmised she now wanted to negotiate. And, not to my surprise she did! "To be honest, I'm looking for something around $30 to $35 an hour. Look, if a company can pay $28.50, what's a few more dollars? "Hah! Don't Make Me Laugh!

Candidates don't understand the concept of job valuation and the planning that goes into setting salaries. But this wasn't a type of discussion to have with a candidate in an interview. "Thelma," I said, "I'm afraid we can't proceed based on several things. Mainly, because you are not satisfied with the salary for the position, and secondly, I do not know if you can even perform the functions of the job. Perhaps this would not be the firm for you." Thelma sensed that her door of opportunity was swiftly closing and said, "Oh, I think I could adjust. Maybe start at the $28.50 and then talk in a month or sooner bout moving it up a little. Sooo, when do ya'll need somebody to start?" My deep, brown African American skin doesn't show color change. So you wouldn't see my skin flush red. Yet, if it were possible, I would have resembled a July 4th fire work event. In the midst of my dismay with Thelma, I had to ask myself, "how did we get here?!" But then Thelma was a presumptuous and very, very ill-prepared candidate.

Interviews generally take 45 minutes to an hour depending on the candidate. Thelma and I now were 15 minutes into the meeting and nothing had been gained in terms of hiring a new employee. I was not interested in this candidate and ready to end the interview. As I sometimes did when time became a factor, I suddenly took a long, theatrical look at my watch. "Oh, goodness. Where does the time go! Thelma, you and I will have to end our interview here. I will get back with you, okay?" I stood, collected my papers and asked Thelma to come with me so I could walk her out. With the same grandeur that she entered is how she left out of the conference room. At the reception, I shook Thelma's hand and was out of sight in seconds. Back in my office, I collapsed in my chair, and raised my arms over my head to ease the tension. William appeared at the door. "So how did that NOT go?" William asked. I smiled, and then jokingly scolded him that he could have given me a warning. I then asked, "Who's next?!"

BASHER AND HER SUPERVISOR

IF YOU DON'T HAVE SOMETHING GOOD to say, it's better to not say anything. That's a motto often heard, right? Yes, of course I'm right. Anyone would be wise to take this principle seriously. Especially during the sacred job interview! At least that was my thinking. And then I met Blanche Mosely.

Blanche was a candidate for the accounting section. The eventual employee would be in the smallest department within the firm. Just the supervisor and two clerks. I always felt accountants were under-appreciated. Accounting is an exact science that tells a story about an entire business operation. Financial charts and graphs sometimes tell a good story or a not so good story about the business operations. On a basic level, accounting reports can demonstrate profit margins, or reflect over-reached expenditures that out-pace budgets due to low projections. Accountants can literally detect and unravel hidden financial data or help bury information. Albeit, an unravelling can, and sometimes does, ultimately bring a company to its demise.

Blanche fit the accounting mold perfectly. She was qualified in every aspect that would bring value to the firm. Talent, a fresh mind of ideas, interpersonal skills, and a professional composure that gave credence to what I hoped to find. Although she was still employed with another firm, Blanche would bring current marketable skills to the table. Just what the firm needed!

Blanche and I met and very quickly relaxed into the interview. Everything was going as anticipated. I explained that I felt we had basically satisfied everything I needed to know. I told her that I had one final question and that I was curious about her relationship with her current supervisor. "Tell me a little about that if you don't mind," I asked her. I felt this would be quick. Blanche would handle the question dutifully as she had so far. I was already forming in my mind who I would assign to her as her mentor and how I would modify her new hire orientation to benefit her most. She would be offered an opportunity with no question. Oh, how I loved to say, "We want to make you an offer of employment with the firm!" So much fun!! Blanche crossed her legs. Her beautiful teal green suit draped her body keeping her perfectly framed as she was seated. She was the epitome of an accountant. Needless to say, it worked for her. "Look, I'm going to be honest with you, okay?" said Blanche. Oh no!! There was that statement, "I'm going to be honest." Of course, I hoped so! Blanche continued by saying, "My supervisor and I—well, we're not cordial. I have a very hard time dealing with her. My work has been sabotaged by her, and frankly, I don't take a lot off her." "O-k-a-y!" This was the last thing I expected. Prompting her further on this, I asked if she could be a little more specific. I told her that not every day is always a good day, however, I wanted her to describe for me why she felt her work was sabotaged. Blanche cleared her throat and dramatically proceeded to respond. Appearing as if someone were forcing her to speak on a witness stand in court, she cusped her hands on top of her knees. She seemed as an actress, who had been asked to re-take her part with hope the second take would be better. "Okay. Well, she said, we had a file management system where we kept accounting data, right?" Was she asking me or telling me—this was really going south fast. I smiled and stated that I supposed so but to keep going. "Well, I prepared the accounting metrics. I worked long hours to get the stats correct and ready. I proofed it and saved the data. The next morning it was due for transmission to headquarters. I sent the report as expected. It was later discovered that the supporting data to the metrics was skewed. The information had been manipulated. I had no idea the report wasn't as I left it. At the time, we didn't have back-end information that revealed the last user who accessed the system. So this left me exposed and with egg on my face. My supervisor is the worse." Hah! Don't make me laugh! At this point, my face had something on it too! The look of bewilderment! I didn't care. "That's an incredible story," I said to Blanche. "Assuming your supervisor was the saboteur, was there ever admission or evidence that she did in fact access the data and sabotage your report?" For my sake, Blanche had to straighten this up so I could feel better about her bashing her supervisor. Blanche's further ill-denouncement about her supervisor never gleaned any clarity. The question here is, "Don't candidates research the pros and cons of interviewing?!" Goodness gracious! For anyone reading this, here's a standard-bearer to interviewing: "Never, ever, speak badly about your present or former employer! There's a real possibility that your current, or former supervisor, and the potential new supervisor could be friends!! It's just bad ethically. Crushed, I said good bye to Blanche, gave her the usual closing that we would be in touch, and thanked her for coming.

CONCLUSION

THE AFORE TOLD INTERVIEW MEMORIES were serious errors in judgment depicting a lack of preparation. There is no such thing as over-preparing. It's like practice makes perfect, right? Yes, of course I'm right. In the current era, there is so much available information to constructively prepare for an interview. The very first step should be to gain as much information about the employer as possible. Familiarize yourself with the names of an employer's agents, administrators, and important business partners. Pronunciation and spelling of these names is also important. You definitely want to pronounce a person's name correctly if you choose to make reference to them in the interview. Study the company's website. Finally, get the location right. Research the distance, and plan the drive time there, where to park, and exactly how to access the interview office site. Sometimes this isn't all that straightforward. You may be planning to park, and stroll in the interview in 5 minutes or less, when actually you have about a 10-15 minute stroll. Again, planning is key.

Something not discussed in any of the interview stories was resumes. A strong recommendation would be to ensure that the resume version provided during the interview mirrors the online submission. If there is an addition, and is a recent enhancement that could not have reasonably been included prior, then definitely include it. Otherwise, hiring managers become skeptical about surprising new revelations or enhancements. But again, if it's justifiable and explainable then by all means add it. Also make sure the resume is accurate, professional and reads well. Some resumes read as though they were lifted directly from the middle of a generic job description. Hiring Managers know the difference. What should be included is direct work experience, for example, current and any former job responsibilities. For example, let's say a person is a manger. As a manger, it is expected that his or her resume would <u>not</u> read like the following:

Responsibilities include supervising departmental staff, implementing administrative systems, planning and directing, and overseeing operations of overall departments within the company.

This is mumble, jumble all run together that reads like it's right out of a generic job description. There is no connectivity to this string of words and frankly puts interviewers to sleep! Or, the resume is skipped over.

It is better to list responsibilities that include accomplishments showing how successfully the person supervised staff or managed a department. A better resume would read something like the following:

- Initiated and assisted in the production of enhanced management for employee evaluation process, resulting in efficiency and accuracy and 50% timesaving.
- Decreased budgetary demands by cutting departmental overtime expenses and scheduling by $50K. Planned and managed $2.5M budget.
- Responsible for unit supervision of 50 field officers.

Now this is something a hiring manager can work with. It tells a story about one's potential and capabilities. Job seekers believe that lifting words from a job description similar to the job they're seeking is adequate. It's not. If a job seeker is serious about getting a job, then it is important to list actual job duties and accomplishments as well as the impact these attributes made. Only then will a resume do its job. Otherwise, Hah! Don't Make Me Laugh!

Wishing you successful interviews that lead to meaningful employment!

So, You Want A Job? Hah! Don't Make Me Laugh!

ABOUT THE AUTHOR

Mamie Gadson grew up in Springfield, Illinois and currently resides in Kingwood, Texas. After a 37-year career in the legal environment, she retired in 2014, as a Human Resources Manager, from the Houston Regional Office of New York based law firm Weil. As a Human Resources Manager, she became a certified Professional in Human Resources (PHR) by the Human Resources Institute of Certification. She was formerly a member of the Society for Human Resources Management (SHRM) and Houston Chapter of HR Houston. As an active member, Mamie was involved in the Legislative Action and Annual Symposium Committees. She was also affiliated with the Houston Chapter of the African American Society of Human Resources Management. As manager, she specialized in talent acquisition and employee relations. She is married 35 years to her husband, Joseph, and they have three daughters, six grandchildren, and two great-grandchildren. Mamie enjoys traveling, and her favorite vacation is to Montecatini Terme, Italy. Mamie finds writing to be exhilarating and delights in sharing her career experiences. "So, You Want A Job? Hah! Don't Make Me Laugh!" is her first book. Although it sometimes reflects a bit of humor, her book aims to enlighten job seekers by understanding how simple mistakes can be detrimental in an interview. Her advice to navigating an interview and becoming triumphant is to prepare. After you've done this, go back and do it again!

Mamie Butler Gadson